# ANGEL'S HEART

## GUIDED BY LIGHT

**LISA**RAY

Ziza Creative
PUBLISHING, INC.

*I lovingly dedicate Angel's Heart Guided by Light
to my late father James Henry Ray (Wray)
aka son, who kept me safe, secure and showered me with love.*

*My beautiful mother Ophelia Esther who loves, cares, and supports me
in everything and who emanates strength and courage.*

*In loving memory of my father-in love, Harold Valle, Sr.*

*To my siblings Anthony Gilbert, Maria, and Jolita for being my protectors.*

*Finally, to my dear son Bryce Devin Valle, who is my heartbeat!
He's witty, smart, and intuitive; I thank God for blessing me
with such light in my life!*

•

*ADDITIONAL THANKS TO
Bishop Caesar and Pastor Bev
Rochelle Miles-Lawley
Loretta Cooky Wisdom
Adelia (Dee-Dee) Johnson
Naomi Caesar Hunter
Liza Barney
Lala Sims
Danielle Durant-Nosworthy
Lisa Joy Page*

# ACKNOWLEDGEMENT & ENDORSEMENTS

I would like to sincerely acknowledge all my family, extended family, friends, and church family who imparted love, confidence and faith into my life. I was impacted in such a way that I have penned this book of poetry as an extension of your love for me. Special acknowledgement goes out to M.S. Finest and M.S. Society. Thank you.

I have had the honor and privilege of knowing Lisa Ray for approximately 25 years. In those years I have known her always to be a person who lives life to the fullest. I have known her as an entrepreneur and entertainer and a fun-loving person having a vibrant joyful spirit that affects everyone around her. She is a beautiful person both inside and out with a welcoming smile that lights up a room. Lisa always strives for excellence in anything she involves herself with and brings to any project the excitement, enthusiasm and a determination to succeed.

For many years I have been blessed to not only be a friend and brother but one of the associate pastors at the church she attends where she is a faithful, committed and a willing worker in many different ministries. I have had the opportunity to watch her as a single mom - love, provide and raise her son Bryce in the fear of the Lord. In recent years Lisa has also been a caregiver for her ailing mom at the same time overcoming physical challenges in her own body. I know that it has been her faith and passionate love for God that has helped her to endure and overcome what many would consider to be insurmountable odds. Her indomitable Spirit has been an inspiration to many. I am certain that this book of poetry will be a blessing to all who read it because it comes from the heart of a woman who has had a real encounter with God and through her experience has learned that even with the many challenges of life one can still live the abundant life that God promises!

*Pastor Alan Plummer*
*Bethel Gospel Tabernacle*

"An eloquent and honest account of life, love and happiness in poetry" – that's how I describe this awesome body of work by Lisa Ray. This book of poetry is a heart-felt, wise, honest, and tender account of someone who has experienced life with pain and spirituality. The poems tell bits and pieces of motherhood, Christianity, faith, loss and love. This epiphany provoking, poetically written book offers insights into how one can live his or her life more fully and derive meaning from life's experiences.

**Lisa J. Page**
*Chief Executive Officer / Omega Training Solutions*

As the Feurtado brothers had the opportunity to sit and speak with Lisa Ray, we found her great passion to see beyond her thought because she realized that to every sleeper there's a dream but to the believer, God gives a vision! Habakkuk 2:3 (KJV) For the vision is yet for an appointed time, but at the end it shall speak, and not lie: though it tarry, wait for it; because it will surely come, it will not tarry.

**Todd & Lance Feurtado**
*King of Kings Foundation*

Lisa Ray's poetry is informed by a life that though well spent, has seen the highs and lows that make it a full life. It is this full life that has given her the perspective of someone who has come full circle and have faced their inner truths.

Her poems are heartfelt and sincere and obviously imbued with her faith yet she avoids being preachy. Her unique syntax and earthy honesty will appeal to a wide range of readers. It is a work that will find its own path in the soulful landscape of personal poetry.

**Kamell Ellis-Chief**
*Marketing Officer / Ellis Enterprises International, Inc.*

These words are a beautiful display of how God bestows upon those who fear Him; beauty for ashes. I have shared my life, which includes my love for Jesus Christ with Lisa Ray, and can testify that He has given her a song of praise to bring glory to His matchless name and a word that will touch the heart of each hearer. There is something so precious about the way she lives her life through her words and these bring healing and hope for all who will have an ear to listen. Reading this book of poems has proven to me that the experiences of her life have given her a reason to rejoice and have displayed His magnificent splendor for all to see!
**Pastor Liza Barney**

Mother's Amazing Love was truly a blessing for me. Having lost a mother, I know all too well how much it is to reminisce about that love. This poem brought back memories and was right on point bringing me to tears of joy and remembrance. Awesome message and much needed, to share about such a beautiful person. Much love to all the moms.
**Danielle Nosworthy**

Mother's Amazing Love, You Hold The Key, and Getting to Know you are three of the many voices of rhyme shared with the world by Lisa Ray, in her new book, *Angel's Heart Guided by Light*. The messages wrapped inside her story is shared easily as she pours from the heart the meaning and sentiment of a voice crying out to share what challenges, benefits and blessings lay in store as we walk through the world. Each person follows the same steps, but none gain the experience through someone else, only through personal commitment. Lisa said: "When I think about amazing love, I think about the love of the Lord, and how He cares and watches over us. But I also think about His wonderful gifts and truly the one that compares to no other is the nurturing unconditional love displayed by a mother..."

In sharing these words of endearment, she showers us with an awareness that we have known but might disregard. In other works included in her book: "Facing resistance after praying for your life, and you pushing back cuts like a knife; because you are still growing and learning. You may not see that I am equipped with wisdom and love inside of me...No one knows the challenges you will face, but I have been in that place." It is indeed difficult to pour out your heart onto a page, but Lisa Ray has done it and enlightens each of us at our point of need. She reaches each reader, as if this message was specified for that person. That is exactly how it should be, and how great writers have accomplished it in years gone by.

Thank you Lisa Ray, My day has been made brighter, and my path clearer, after sharing your wisdom in these pages.
*Don Durant*

# INTRODUCTION

### Discovering MS

After having back surgery, the Lord spoke to me in my bed of affliction and it was then that I said, "I'm giving it all up for you Lord. Show me what you want me to do and I'll do it!" It not about me, it's about Him. When you come to the end of yourself, you come into a true relationship with Jesus Christ. I came to the realization that God has blessed me and kept me my whole life! Yes I've made mistakes being disobedient and turning away from God. But His love kept me, He proved Himself over and over again; through loss of my dad who was my greatest inspiration as a child. Overcoming adversity, growing up with a dysfunctional family plagued with addiction to drugs, alcohol, and mental illness. My Lord and Savior kept me and through it all; I felt His love and presence. Just as I vowed to raise my son Bryce to know Him; I vowed to be a willing vessel for His Kingdom and His glory, by operating in the gifts He has given me to encourage, empower and be of service to God's people. His plan and His purpose be done.

*-Jeremiah 29:11*


### Living with MS

I want to share the Love of God with people. My experience with MS does not overtake me because of my faith. I believe in miracles because I believe in Christ and He has provided and kept me. When I am weak, He is strong. So for those who are suffering in silence, I want them to know there is hope for overcoming MS through Christ. Trust in the Lord with all your heart and lean not on your own understanding. Choose life, choose Jesus Christ! It gets better and I am determined to be a witness and help those in need. I choose to be transparent and choose to live. To live is Christ, try Him.

# FOREWORD

Words. Phrases. Expressions. Thoughts. Insights. Feelings, and I could go on and on with this list. Poetry is a wonderful, creative expressive forum to share opinions and feelings through words. And not just any words but words that can take you on a journey through the mind's eye. Words and phrases that express emotions, feelings, insights, and opinion bringing one to a place of peace, joy, excitement, sadness, comfort, hope, and so on.

Poetry can be rhythmically therapeutic, spiritually awakening, politically challenging, socially empowering and personally engaging. Poetry comes in all shapes and sizes. There are over 50 types of poems - to name just a few styles that you will encounter in Lisa's book: Sonnet, Limerick, Haiku, Narrative, Epic, Couplet, Free Verse, Acrostic, Ballad.

In this book of poetry, you will be delightfully entertained as you wrap your mind around the words and verses expressed within these pages.

As this millennial generation searches for direction and answers to this complex world, many reach out through poetry to express their frustrations, hurts, disappointments and unanswered questions. Many of their words are dark and filled with hate. Others use this medium to reach inside themselves and find a peace that this world cannot give them. They find that Jesus Christ is indeed the answer for their challenges. Using the medium, as Lisa does, they are able to express their findings through great inspirational poetry that points the way to true satisfaction of the soul.

Lisa has done just that through her poems! As you read you will certainly attain satisfaction of the soul.

**Beverly Morrison Caesar**

# TABLE OF CONTENTS

# GOD SPEAKS

# AWAKENING

I feel like I've had an awakening. I trust God and I fear Him. My desire is to please Him. I have enjoyed many things in my life and did things my way. Selfish thinking only concerned about what was on my plate. Now after so many years of God sparing my life I get it. Seek Him first to do His will and all good things will be added unto you. He is and has been providing for me not because I deserve it but because He loves me. That's the kind of Love I need and the kind of love I want to give. My labor is unto the Lord. I follow Him no more mistakes can I afford. Tell everyone how Great He is and to follow His precepts and know they are His. Happiness and joy will consume you as you surrender to a love so awesome and tender. Oh the peace knowing Jesus doubt will cease. Rest in His word for He is Lord! Hail to the King creator of you and me. There is no time for faking! I just experienced an awakening!

# YOU NEVER LEFT

*You never left me and you allowed me to go my own way. Lord You kept me and now I'm down on my knees once again. Your love is all over me, the love you have for me I will never forget. Oh how you set me free and I know you're not done with me yet. I've changed on the inside, no I'm not the same, you heard my cry and I know you were with me all the way and this time I'm not going my own way. It's your way I'm not going mine anymore. It's your way thank you for knocking at my door. It's your way, there's no other way but the way of the Lord!*

# YOU ENLIGHTEN ME

You enlighten me because you are the light.
You are my source the great director who gives hope to the lost.

Those who seek you seek your heart starting with trust through
the wisdom you impart. Gaining understanding with each trial
I face. Knowing it's you who have equipped me to win the race.
I say win because with you there is no losing, so I focus on you
and you made this choice free! But it's free for everyone not
just free for me. There's none like you, you give strength to the
weak and knowing you is love. Knowing you brings peace. So
I'm thankful for your will for me, for direction, and purpose you
enlighten me!

# STILL SMALL VOICE

There's a still small voice living inside my heart I know
He orders my steps and directs me everywhere I go
His Love is amazing and there's no one like the Great I AM
I would be crazy not to trust Him my life in His hands
He has the Master plan

You are Alpha and Omega oh Lord the beginning and the end
You gave up your life at Calvary so I can live again
Life is not at a loss
Because you hung on the cross
You paid the price the ultimate sacrifice
And now I know I have eternal life
Thanks for being near
and letting me hear...
...Your still small voice.

## OVERFLOW

There's an overflow in my belly causing me not to sleep
About to burst because I'm ready to hear what God speaks.
There is an overflow of vision in my head
And I can't stop writing exactly what God said.

Nudging and tugging at my spirit
God is speaking to me and I hear it!
But it's not for me it's for His people at large.
I am being obedient as I listen to His charge.
He said my people need to know who I Am
so I'm using your life as witness to show them they can...

...rely on Me, trust Me, serve Me, and love Me.

When they choose to give me their life,
I will direct their path because I AM the LIGHT!

*God is speaking to me and I hear it!*

# TRANSFORMATION

# GETTING TO KNOW YOU AND WHOSE I AM

*Learning to accept that you have a purpose and a plan. Pushing past what I see and think, doing what I must do even when I don't understand. Giving You honor in my triumphs and overcoming trials - because you told me I can.*

You are the very beat of my heart because of Your Love.
I'm living in righteousness and You're the reason because...
You created the world, and included me still...
I came in sin but now I seek your will.

There's been pain, heartache, persecution too.
But I've learned lessons and above all I'm getting to know You!
It's amazing on how it has taken so long,
but with no regrets and I'm still holding on.

Almighty, All Knowing that's who You are...
...and I trust You for everything I was created to be,
not because I'm worthy but because You chose me.
As I continue to grow and trust you too,
I take pleasure in getting to know You!

*I'm living in righteousness and You're the reason because...*

# PAUSED!

My life has been put on pause in a sense.
To get closer to God, yes closer to Him.

My days now are longer than my nights
I'm happy at home without a fuss or a fight.
Now I spend quality time with Him at home.
It's a Blessing having Him with me, I'm not alone.

I grow stronger in Him daily, God builds me up!
Providing all my needs and strengthening me with His Love.

I'm chasing after the heart of God,
pursuing my purpose for His Kingdom.
Trusting His Holy Spirit for discernment and wisdom.
My faith is in Jesus and continues to increase
While I go through the trials, my God gives me peace.

And in these trials there's joy in my heart
As the Master is at work perfecting what He started.
So trust me it's good to follow His Laws
and I'm happy He's keeping me while my life is on pause.

# ORDERED STEPS

God just stopped me, dead in my tracks...
        Not to punish me, but to make sure I didn't turn back.

Back into chains of the past that had me bound.
        He's given me a purpose and had me write it down.
        *(Something I could refer to, reflect on and plan.)*

You see He's been speaking to me for quite some time,
        But I was always too busy with worldly things on my mind.

God never gave up and speaks to me still,
        Now I am stable and seeking His will.

Every trial I face there have been lessons learned -
- and I've always been kept.
        I finally get it...God has ordered my steps.

You never know who's watching you -
-so make sure you are salt and light!
      Stay on your knees, seek God and pray with all your might.

To stay in the race, pray without ceasing.
        Have faith in the Lord, pray and you'll please Him!

You must trust God to keep you even if you are not there yet.
        Remember God is infinite in wisdom, in love -
        - and He has ordered your steps!

# EMBRACING GOD'S PURPOSE

It's okay that you didn't throw a football. That was not your bag.
You did not gravitate to basketball, creativity is what you had.
Strong willed and smart as a little boy and now a man,
Knowing nothing is impossible and saying, "God with me I can."
Your foundation is in Christ thank God He saved us.
In fact, He has great plans for you and great purpose.
The world is dysfunctional seems without direction,
But God loves you so much and gave you gifts of perfection.
A wonderful caring person, who's made mistakes,

but you're not alone -

We have all fallen short but God keeps us close to home.

Never doubt what you've been taught or how rough the road can be,
just know the Blood of Jesus covers you and you are free.

*He forgives and has paid the price for our sins, through His blood bought sacrifice.*

Stand on His promises and affirm:
**"I know who I am & whose I am."**

*More than a conqueror, coming through the storm, because God is with me,*
His purpose is being realized through the test.
In fact, as I come through I'm better, heading to my best.

Now I can help you young person who has been hurt and broken
My family I am a support for, from the wife I will meet and in time my children.

Embracing God's Purpose

# I WILL NEVER BE DEFEATED

I will never be defeated when I trust you.
My life's purpose is completed when I trust you
I never have to worry about what people say or what they do.
Because I have victory in Jesus! Yes I do.
As a child I did as children do.
Went to school, had fun and listened to my parents too.
Now I'm all grown up living my life and raising a family too.
I get through life's trials because of Christ too.
Yes I have victory in Jesus! Yes I do.
Never be disappointed when I have you
Walking in your anointing because of you.
I never have to worry about what people say or what they do
'cause I have victory in Jesus! Yes I do!
If I need some direction I trust you.
Your wisdom is perfect and everything you do.
So I'm loving my life serving you,
I trust you and I have victory in Jesus! Yes I do!

Now I'm older and I'm wiser with responsibility.
I'm walking in promises that God has for me.
No matter what my ears hear or what my eyes see.
I know I have victory in Jesus. Victory for me.

*Oh you never know who's watching you*
*So be sure to walk in the light*
Make sure it's Jesus people see
So they can see the victory.

Victory in Jesus!

# DON'T WALK ALONE

*It's foolish to walk without direction,*
*Where are you going, do you have a plan?*
*Walk in the way of the Lord and He will direct your path.*

Along the way you may stumble and fall,
But He will be with you just answer His call

*Learn His voice with discipline and obedience*
*Read His word it is time well spent*

That time you freely give to Him seeking His face
Will keep you covered with His Blood Mercy and Grace!

The answers to all the questions in your heart
Are there in His word the best place to start

Oh yes one other thing you should learn how to pray
God loves an Intercessor so pray every day

In fact pray all the day for others and yourself
He will give you what you need He's your source He's your help!

*Where are you going?*
*Do you have a plan?*

# CHERISHING MOM

# MOTHER'S AMAZING LOVE

When I think about amazing love I think about the love of the Lord and how he cares and watches over us. But I also think about His wonderful gifts and truly the one that compares to no other is the nurturing unconditional love displayed by a mother.

A mother's love is selfless, genuine, and kind and she is always doing things with her children on her mind. Never considering what her needs would be, she is focused on guiding you to succeed in who God made you to be.

A mother gives you hugs and kisses to ease the pain and the sun shines through her smile, even when it rains. A mother is someone you know you can trust and when you're down you yearn to have mom around. Through life's ups and downs she is understanding. She displays strength, patience, and love, but is never too demanding.

Let's be clear, she is no push over and manages many lives, besides her title is mother. Amazing mothers are there to wipe away the tears and they seem to be invincible when they ease our sense of fear.

She always has time, when there is none. She always has food for everyone. She has band-aids for cuts and bruises, and will make you feel like a winner, when others say that you're a loser. Her heart is sincere and pure too. But she never seems to get the credit that she is due. One day is not sufficient to acknowledge your life. You've given so much of yourself through love and sacrifice.

I'm so thankful mom introduced me to the Lord above. But I am especially thankful to God for mother's amazing love. I am blessed to have you and I rejoice because of your life. Please know that you are loved, and your true reward is the Love of Christ! Mother's Amazing Love.

# MOMMY

Mommy we are so different, but in many ways the same.
I have your eyes, your smile, and I often feel your pain.

I remember how happy you were, when I was a child.
You planned parties, dressed us up, and always with a smile.

Today I see sadness in your eyes and wonder why.
How could someone so loving and beautiful experience sadness
and cry.

I love you so much mommy and it hurts me to see you in pain.
I pray God brings you joy and happiness again.

*God makes the impossible possible, so I trust and believe.*
*God please touch my mother's mind, let her know she is loved.*
*God please give my mom peace.*

Turn her life around to experience Your joy!
Let her enjoy her grandchildren and great grands,
the girls and the boys!

God You are our Father, You are love.
Touch my mom, my mother with your love from above.

Oh Jesus, remember my mommy.

*I have your eyes, your smile,*
*and I often feel your pain.*

# I LOVE THE MOTHERS
# AND THEIR LOVE

Mothers stand close to their families tight like a glove. Always ready to inspire and encourage and if necessary chastise. She's doing God's work from her heart for everyone who hurts and those who cry. You don't have to be family a stranger will do but she has love and compassion for you too! Sometimes I feel alone, hurt in need of a hug, one from a mother who displays real love.

The love given to us by Jesus that lets us know it's okay.
So, it may be your mother or mine but mother...
                                    she is always ready to stay and pray.
There's something about her touch and nurturing care.
She makes you feel safe just knowing she's there.
I thank God for moms always gentle and kind.
Praying diligently for us with God in her heart and mind!

# LOVE MY MOMMY

My mommy is the sweetest Woman I know
She's so beautiful inside out, and full of wisdom,
strength and love no doubt.
You see mommy has been through so much hurt and pain
That many times I wondered if she'd see happiness again
I would give up all I had to see mommy happy and not feeling sad
Not looking alone or feeling unloved, mommy I love you so much
How can I help you feel that again
After so much hurt, heartache and pain
Truth be told God made you so beautiful
You are so much like Him giving of yourself
Thinking of others and loving unconditionally
The lessons you've taught know no boundaries or color
Just warmth, love and understanding of a true mother
Mommy I love you!!

*The lessons you've taught
know no boundaries or color.*

# LOVE PETALS

# PICTURES OF YOU

When I see pictures of you now it hurts,

All I can remember are your last words.

Your smile reminds me of the good times we had,

But at the same time it makes me sad.

It actually brings tears to my eyes

Because you flipped the script and I still don't know why.

Bottled up feelings tossed aside,

Asking myself over and over, was it all lies?

You see I was for real make no mistake about it.

I never knew that you had started to doubt it.

And because I cannot share with you how I feel,

I have to write it down, so I can heal.

Life goes on and we both still have to work,

But it's just harder for me because I'm still hurt!

WOW - pictures of you!

*Bottled up feelings tossed aside,
asking myself over and over, was it all lies?*

# PARTS OF YOU I LOVE

There are parts of you I love, I mean I adore.
It touches my heart and I desire more.
But there are things you do that I seem to hate,
But because I love you, I tolerate...it

Yes I know hate is a strong word to describe
                    and I don't harbor any in my heart.
But to think about the things we put up with, just to be a part

I know there are things about me that you don't like,
but if we sat down and talked about it...I could change, I might.

Sometimes I wonder what's the point with matters of the heart...
Seems like we always end up back where we started
                              *...alone, maybe?*

The moral of the story is you can't help who you love,
just maybe it would be different if it came from up above.

WOW, there are parts of you I love!

# DISTANT LOVE

I guess I'll love you at a distance
Because we don't see eye to eye
Although there are some things we want together
There are others you don't care to try

It's important to be honest
When you're in pursuit
To fit into an equation of
1 + 1 makes two

I felt a spiritual connection
Thought we could be together in time
Suddenly out of nowhere
You decided to change your mind

I'll miss talking, laughing, dancing
Spending time holding hands
Going back to pushing forward
Because God has greater plans

So, as disappointed as I am
Know I was willing to take a chance *(on love)*
But now that you have given up
I'll love you at a distance.

## MISSING LOVE

Sometimes it's hard being away from you
I just want to see your face
Instead I have to look at a picture of you in it's place
Don't get me wrong I'm happy I have it while I wait
But ain't nothing like the real thing and for that there's no debate
There's always love's passion in everything I say
Praying for you every day for God to keep you safe
Never bad intentions not trying to make a fuss
I thought you should know my heart misses you so much.

*xoxo*

*It's important to be honest
when you're in pursuit...*

# ALL EYES ON YOU

## JOPPA LEADER

Maybe a child watched you from a distance
as you took your place one Sunday.
They wanted to be there as you shared the good news,
and they knew they would one day.
As you taught the Gospel with wisdom and sincerity;
sharing from God's word on their level for clarity.

Noticing the son or daughter not paying attention,
so you walked over touched a shoulder saying,
"did you hear what I mentioned?"
As a young person you are important to me,
you are important to the Lord!
So you continue to share God's goodness
and now you are all on one accord.
You never gave up on the young person sitting in the back,
instead asked him to move forward to help keep them on track.

You see it was their turn to hear about Christ
and how life without Him is lost!
So you watched, encouraged, and prayed to teach them,
in fact reach them at any cost.
You know the price for our sins was already paid.
You are now a witness to these beginners
we are all sinners saved by grace.
You trusted God who equips you and is your Keeper.
Lean on Him as He guides with His Heart
to serve young people...Joppa leader!
Teaching young men and women to value
their lives and serve Jesus Christ!

## HEARTS TALK

Have you ever had a talk with yourself?
Communicated with your heart and said exactly how you felt
Not able to speak your mind for fear of being rejected
Holding thoughts inside your mind knowing you've been neglected
Trying to sort through mistakes and decisions you've made
Experiencing pain as the outcome but knowing you'll be okay
Knowing you are not perfect always fighting within
Yet praying to JEHOVAH again and again
As you push forward with trust exercising your faith
Expecting victory as God's creation because what HE makes is Great!
This is your life and how you've been taught,
So know God lives in you, so have a hearts talk!

## CELEBRATE YOU

*Sincere, giving, loving and kind*
*Always putting others first with a Christ-like mind*
*Thoughtful and living life on purpose*
*Today is your day and we celebrate you because you're worth it*
*Thank you for caring and loving all of us*
*Always planning and preparing and thinking*
*Of how you can be a blessing.*
*In fact what you don't realize is your life has blessed us all.*
*So on your special day, this milestone embrace and enjoy,*
*Better yet have a ball.*

# CALLED TO LEAD

*In honor of Pastor Roderick Caesar, III*

I've been called to lead you, now will you pray?
You see I answer to God as He prepares me on what to say
I am committed to live holy and be an example to you all
While it is a part of my history, my legacy,
                                    it is in fact an answered call

Obedience is better than sacrifice
And I choose to serve King Jesus
He paid the price giving His life
So life would be better, yes eternal for us

I was raised right here in Bethel - the house of God,
A vision founded by my grandfather Bishop Roderick Senior,
                              who planted and taught you well.
So much so many would excel in God.
                    In fact my dad followed *him*, as *he* followed *Christ*
Bishop Roderick number two for many years he served us too.

        "Now we are here for all to see the legacy continue...
    with Pastor Roderick Caesar III making it three times,
        how nice. So let's rejoice and continue to pray."

I've been called to lead you and God makes a way.

# SPIRITUAL DAD

I attended your church after an invitation,
      when I finally came it was a wonderful experience, in fact
                                amazing!

You spoke the word God had given,
      but even more than that I could see you were living.

Living a life on purpose, encouraging others,
           helping us to know we are worth it
That our lives were meaningful because God created us
More importantly as believers He lives in us.

You are a gentleman like Him, loving, humble,
           and for Jesus always ready to work.
Trusting the call on your life, even when challenged or hurt.
Your character speaks for itself, a life well lived,
             and always a present help.

We look to you as you look to Christ,
      and it helps us to be better, which is really quite nice .
Please know that we watch, listen,
         read and study God's word as you direct us.
We hear your voice as a reminder our Bishop

Knowing to live beneath our means and to always speak life.
   Bishop Caesar who leads by example, the example of Christ!

So thank you Bishop for sharing your life,
         and giving us all you had

We love, respect, and appreciate you, our Spiritual Dad.

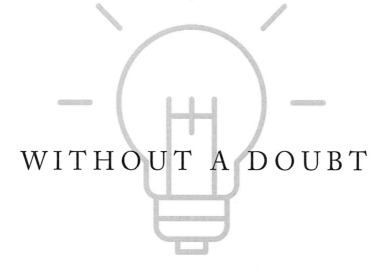

WITHOUT A DOUBT

# GOD IS SO GOOD!

God is so good when I lost my job money was still coming in. He put food on the table and He paid my rent.

Not one time did I have to go into my savings except when He told me to plant a seed. Shortly after that He made a way for a job that was in need.

Let me tell you how good God is...when the job let me go in August and benefits done in 30 days, He sent me to the doctor to make sure I was okay.

To my surprise a polyp on my womb and a lump on my breast the doctors did find. Then two surgeries in two weeks and the results were benign!

Do you see how good He is? My faith has increased and I trust Him more because I believe.

I can't keep His love a secret I think of Him all the time. His Grace is sufficient, He's yours and He's mine!

It's been a year, and I still believe God for the right position! In the meantime He's keeping me and I thank Him for the Blessing! God is so good!

# SOMETIMES YOU HAVE TO CRY

*Sometimes you have to cry to sort things out.*
To see all the possibilities and eliminate doubt

*Turn away from negativity and get rid of stress.*
Dig deep in your soul and pull out your best!

*Time's not on your side, but God truly is*
And you can experience His goodness once you know you're His.

*So move on, press forward, never give up, always try...*
your best and you'll get by.

*When life's trials come your way and the load is too much to bear*
And you feel all alone like there's no one who cares.

*Don't throw up your hands and try to understand why.*
Just pull it together with your tears and know -
***Sometimes you have to cry.***

*Time's not on your side, but God truly is.*

WAR

# DAVID BATTLES

I was lost in a confused state of mind
But the king had me covered under His Blood all the time
Of course I didn't know it
Over and over I had to blow it
My Spirit constantly battling my flesh
Little did I know I was in a mess
Give up my life, but at what cost
I know I belong, just right now I'm lost

*All the Lord was waiting for was a YES*

Yes to Your will, Yes to Your way
Then off again I go putting salvation off for another day.

*Give up my life, but at what cost*
*I know I belong, just right now I'm lost...*

# WOMAN'S BEAUTY

*Is your heart really in it? I mean can you really get with this?*
Or maybe it just feels convenient, but doesn't quite fit.


*Do you have the patience to put up with a relationship?*
Can you understand commitment doesn't mean throw your
hands up and just quit?


*After all these years and all this time,*
You are still battling demons and can't make up your mind.


*Thinking you could find something better!*
But don't you know, no one is ever that clever.


*One day by God's grace you'll become old,*
Prayerfully realizing what you had was more precious than
gold.


*Men always love beauty on the outside no doubt,*
But the true beauty of a woman is inside out.


*So don't judge a book by its cover, you may be fooled by what you see.*
The real beauty is when you discover the God in me.

# WAR [WOMEN ARE READY]

Women are ready to stand in the midst of adversity
and not go our own way.
We stand on our faith and get on our knees and pray.

We dodge the bullets, slings, and snares we face in our lives
Because of the Blood of the Lamb Jesus Christ!
The weapons of our warfare are not carnal,
But built by His Spirit is how we battle.

The battle is not ours, it's the Lords,
But He has equipped us with His word, our sword!
If you knew Him like we do, you too would be in awe
And we stand in position as we battle **WAR**.

Women Are Ready!

*I'm staying in tune and keeping it real...*

## YOUR WILL

I'm walking in my healing
**In expectation of full restoration**
Not down and out because of this trial
**Learning lessons through confession and with a smile.**
Realizing that without you I cannot live but merely exist
**But you chose me, you saved me and I stand on your promise**
Knowing You at times is surreal
**As I embrace your grace and do Your will**
I'm happy knowing Your grace is enough
**And I love you knowing You love me so much!**
So I'm staying in tune and keeping it real
**As you guide me I do not mine... but Your will!**

# EVER AFTER

# WINGS

*I bet you didn't think I could fly,*
But it was destined for me since birth
God held on to my wings
Since He placed me here on Earth
My life had meaning
And He gave me purpose
To raise my beautiful girl
Who He graciously blessed me with
God gave me life
And put you all in my life to love
Know that I'll love you forever
As I rest with Him above

*I bet you didn't know I could fly – you may be sad and wonder why*
*Why it hurts so much when you lose someone you love*

I love you so much
You have to know that from the start
So when you think of me, smile
And keep me close in your heart
In Spirit I will be with you always
So please don't cry
I'm no longer suffering, I have peace
And the Lord has given me wings and I CAN FLY!

# REFLECTIONS

You must have known today would be tough to face, because you're not around. I thought by now it would be easier getting through a tough time, figuring out a problem, or enjoying a holiday without you.

The truth is sometimes I have a moment when I feel alone, although there are people around me. I still miss you and that's the truth and yes Holidays are quite different without you.

There was something about your smile and the laughter you let out in the atmosphere. You made everything so special with the joy you brought to our lives. We always knew you cared.

You must have seen the tears in today, because I suddenly felt you near. You must have felt the pain in my heart, because suddenly the phone rang. You had to know I needed something special, a little hug to know I'm loved. You showed up once again just in time my angel from above.

Things are quite different I know, but I remember the great times we had. The best part of it all is I know God is watching over me. He is my father and so is my Dad.

# DADDY'S GIFT

My Dad raised me to know Him at a young age.
Life was beautiful although at times I saw rage.
Daddy did his best to make sure
We had all we needed to endure
This life's ups and downs challenges we faced,
But properly prepared to endure the race
He shared God's love and taught us about mercy and grace
He knew we needed that to stare evil in the face

Suited up with nurturing love and wisdom, and faith in God
Was the seed planted and understanding wasn't that hard
Given a foundation that I stand on today
Even though Daddy's gone, he passed away
I know that I will see him again someday
God made it so because of salvation, He made it that way!

Dad left me with a gift I'll have forever and it's the best!
Daughter you're never alone your Father is with you -
**His name is Jesus!**

# REFLECTION OF DAD'S JOURNEY

Just like a father who delights in His son
Sharing your love for others as God did His Son!

Sacrificing time, providing support in all you do
Giving of yourself, sharing wisdom too

Talented beyond measure, story teller and poet
Yes played the piano too and many don't know it

When you'll get your wings, no one knows
You live you die that's how the story goes

But what have you done in between
You've touch the lives of others with your soul and your being

You lived a full life with integrity and passion
Always ready to spring into action...*for a cause*

Family or friends you treated us with love and respect
Always showed up and stayed on the set

You loved your grandchildren and adored your son
A humble man who showed love to everyone

Thank you for all you've done and for all your love
Now resting with the father in heaven above.

WAKE UP

# CONSIDERING NEW THINGS

I'm considering new things
*now that my Spirit is awake*

Now thinking of writing down
*what would be perfect in a mate.*

I'm considering searching my soul
*now that emotions have been stirred.*

To make sure what I get in life
*is what I deserve.*

Tired of going in circles-
*one day up, next day down.*

Still trying to find my way
*to a place that's safe and sound.*

I'm considering helping others
*who have been pushed, who have been shoved*

And letting them know they are special
*and letting them know they are loved.*

Trying to understand why
*I still didn't get it quite right.*

I'm leaning on the Lord
*and praying with all my might.*

Yes I'm considering new things
*thanking God with all my heart.*

For His many Blessings
*and giving me a brand new start!*

*I'm considering new things!*

# LIFE CHANGES

Sometimes life changes **slap you right in the face!**
Have you ever felt like the **rug was pulled from underneath?**

Suddenly you're not sure how you're going to eat...
....make ends meet and you can't sleep!
That's why we have to keep on our shield of faith
and know our mere existence is not a mistake.

The devil is always on attack and after you,
but power and authority is yours because of Christ in you.
Oh it gets hard and friends will become clear
                              even if many,
                              a few,
                              some,
                              or just one!

Life changes can throw you for a loop,
but we overcome by our testimonies or our test
and when you come through the storm you've done your best!
But what's next?
Life changes!

# IT'S TIME

With me you were consistent, at least in MY mind.
Was it just for fun and now you thinking IT'S TIME?

It's time to keep pushing on, although I thought you would be there,
But to my surprise you just don't seem to care.

Nothing is ever perfect, relationships take a little work.
It's all about give and take, but not taking until it HURTS!

When faced with a bump in the road, you could have talk to me,
To sort it out because we care. Instead you chose to flee.

You said it was risk and I obviously was blind,
To think we were into each other. I guess it was all in my mind.

It may have been nothing to you, but to me it was a start.
The start of something beautiful...sharing Love from my heart.

Oh yeah, you had me going, but I deserve the best...
I know God is still with me and He hasn't failed me yet.

Whatever your reasons were...I CANNOT read YOUR mind.
I wish you would have told me that...it's over, it's done...IT'S TIME.

*Wounded

# PAY ATTENTION
## *WHAT HAPPENED TO YOU?*

To me you were such a nice surprise, someone special to be mine
You seemed sincere to me you were so kind
You held secrets to get close to me always acting like you care
perhaps for selfish reasons I thought you would be there
I thought you would love me from your heart
Instead you came with drama and left me some scars
You never gave me a choice to make decisions on my own
Suddenly out of nowhere you made the truth known
I should listen to God's voice each time I hear
He is always truthful always sincere
You should have been real you should have been true.
Nothing but lies what happened to you!

*You should have been real*
*you should have been true.*

# OUR LIVES MATTER

# AS I GROW

There is beauty in the world, I'm happy I'm free
I will not allow you to step on me
No pumped up egos I'm following my dream
Knowing I'm with it, confident with self esteem

YOU ARE SPECIAL AND UNIQUE
LOOK IN THE MIRROR AND TELL ME WHAT YOU SEE

A miracle so precious not just a child
A vision so wonderful especially when you smile
Your name identifies purpose and always a reason
An opportunity to blossom like a flower in season
Embrace your differences, open your eyes, don't be blind
And whatever you do, don't forget to be kind.

# 1WORLD

My complexion doesn't matter or the language that I speak
And You shouldn't judge me on my ethnicity

You see I was created to be unique
Outside beauty reflected and on the inside of me
Full of love and passion to be the best I can be
I appreciate you, So why not appreciate me

We are all 1World a part of the human race
Wherever you are, whatever you do, there will be things
You don't want to face

1World no hate limitless in love
1World embracing our sons and daughters, resist useless chatter
1World of peace because all lives do matter

Let's use wisdom, understanding and knowledge too
1World represents me and 1World represents you.

# FACING RESISTANCE

Facing resistance after praying for your life
and you pushing back cuts like a knife.
Because you're still growing and learning you may not see,
That I am equipped with wisdom and love inside of me.
No one knows the challenges you will face.
But I'll tell you a secret I've been in that place.
Thinking I knew better than what my mom shared with me.
Now I appreciate her and finally see,
All the love and sacrifice she made for my life.
Now I'm on the right path living for Christ.
So you and I are not perfect, but one thing for sure
I tell the hard truth because for you I want more.
I belong to Him and so do you,
And I trust in His promises that's what I do.
So I face resistance day after day,
But I'll face it with love and on my knees as I pray!

*No one knows the challenges you will face*
*But I'll tell you a secret I've been in that place.*

# YOU HOLD THE KEY

*You hold the key to unlock your past*
To the history of our ancestors who set the path

*The very thing you have a knack for gives a glimpse of who they were,*
but more importantly shares a story of who you are

*You are a Prince, a Princess, a King or a Queen.*
So hold on be proud of your heritage be proud of your being

*Stand on the shoulders of the great men and women and don't lose sight*
of the oppression they suffered or fight for civil rights

*Yes walk with your head up high*
stay grounded and look to the heavenly sky

*Doing your best will allow others to share in your joy.*
Know that you are special young girl and young boy

*You have a legacy and a purpose Black Woman, Black man*
So continue to dream and stay focused on the plan

*You hold the key that unlocks the past.*

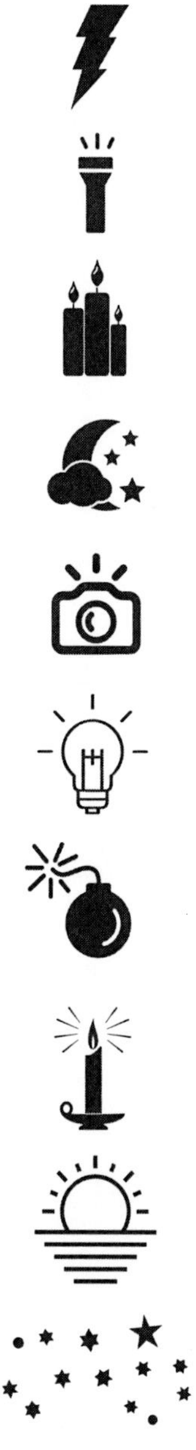

**LISA & SON, BRYCE**
*THROUGH THE YEARS*

*A miracle so precious not just a child*
*A vision so wonderful especially when you smile*

*- As I Grow, Page 68*

TOP: AUNTIE RUBY, MOM (OPHELIA) & BABY LISA
BOTTOM: LISA & MOM, OPHELIA

*A mother's love is selfless, genuine, and kind*
*and she is always doing things with her children on her mind.*
*Never considering what her needs would be,*
*she is focused on guiding you to succeed in who God made you to be.*

- *Mother's Amazing Love*, Page 28

### LISA'S PARENTS
*JAMES HENRY & OPHELIA ESTHER*

*You hold the key to unlock your past*
*To the history of our ancestors who set the path*

*- You Hold The Key, Page 71*

# ABOUT THE AUTHOR

*I can do all things through Christ who strengthens me!*

Lisa Angel Ray born March 22, 1965 to a Puerto Rican mother Ophelia from Spanish Harlem and an African American father James with Jamaican roots from Georgia and raised on 160 street in South side Jamaica, Queens. Lisa affectionately known as TaTa to close family and friends is the youngest child and has two sisters and one brother. As a little girl Lisa wrote poetry and in second grade was chosen to recite a poem for Senator Shirley Chisholm. She attended PS 45, Junior HS IS72 and August Martin HS where she graduated in 1982. She started working on wall street that same year and took some college courses. By 1986 she recorded two singles with a group and quickly realized how male dominated the music business was and it was unfavorable for women with morals and values. In 1989 she established an entertainment company and served as president until 1997, at which time she went back to school. In 2005, Lisa graduated with a 3.91 GPA from St. John's University receiving an Associates Degree. On July 19th she gave birth to a bouncing baby boy Bryce Devin Valle who she promised to raise in Christ! She prayed for her son and his salvation and God has truly blessed her saving young Bryce at just six years old.

In 2010 she was laid off and has since had three surgeries. She attributes all that she has to Jesus. Lisa loves children and helping people and is believing God for a husband, but in the meantime she is happy serving Him! "God is my provider and my source and I am pleased He allowed me to return to school, to change careers, to help others, and lead them to Christ!" -Lisa

*"For I know the plans I have for you," declares the LORD, "plans to prosper you and not to harm you, plans to give you hope and a future." Jeremiah 29:11*

CONNECT WITH LISA: FACEBOOK.COM/LISA.RAY.7106 • IG : @THEREAL_LISARAY

$10.00

ISBN 978-0-692-11700-2

51000>